THE MEANWOOD VILLAGE ASSO

MEANWOO
IN
PICTURES

The oldest known photograph of Meanwood, taken from a lantern slide by J.W.Ramsden about 1852, in the very early days of photography. The old fire-damaged paper mill, the dam, Church, original Chapel, Brick Row and Dagless's farm can be discerned.

VOLUME I — 1852 to the 1960s

Compiled by
PETER BEWELL

Assisted by
BRYN EVANS, ARTHUR HOPWOOD and DOREEN WOOD

Published by
M.V.A. Publications

95, Green Road
Meanwood
Leeds LS6 4LE

First published 2004
Reprinted 2005, 2011

ISBN 978 0 9547946 0 6

Printed and bound by
Smith Settle Printing and Bookbinding Ltd
Gateway Drive, Yeadon, West Yorkshire LS19 7XY

MEANWOOD

"The Village within a City"

Meanwood is now a dormitory suburb of the great City of Leeds in West Yorkshire, but in the times covered by the pictures in this book, it was a working village inhabited by quarrymen, tanners, fellmongers, papermakers, millers and, to a small extent, farmers. Before then the area around the Myrtle and Parkside Road was known as High Meanwood or Meanwood Hilltop, and the lower part of the valley around Green Road and Hustler's Row Meanwoodside or Woodside.

The earliest references to Meanwood (spelt in various ways) go back to the thirteenth century, when the monks of Kirkstall Abbey were granted land in the area and established a corn mill on the local beck. Anyone interested in the history should read the excellent book by Arthur Hopwood and Fred Casperson simply entitled "Meanwood" and first published in 1986. (see inside back cover)

As well as humble workers' cottages there were also a number of fine houses such as Meanwood Hall, Meanwoodside (sadly demolished in the 1950s), Carr Manor, Meanwood Towers, Alder Hill and Hollin House and all of these feature in the book.

Meanwood has long been a favourite area for walkers, being situated at the terminus of the old tram route. It is an excellent starting point for walks along the "Meanwood Valley Trail" to the Seven Arches, Adel Crag, and Golden Acre Park. The more adventurous can even carry on to the Lake District via the "Dales Way" long-distance footpath.

In years past it was also a favourite Sunday afternoon walk for the people of Woodhouse who came over the parkland known as Woodhouse Ridge with its neatly laid out footpaths, shelters and bandstand, and down into the valley.

The wooded valley is still a beautiful area and the home of foxes, badgers, herons, kingfishers and many other animals and birds.

We have tried to show a wide selection of buildings and places in the book and have not stuck rigidly to the parish boundary. There are various group photographs, and many readers will no doubt take pleasure in spotting themselves, friends and relatives amongst them. Others may well enjoy seeing the old fashioned clothing.

As you will see towards the end of the book, the demolition craze of the 1960s and 70s struck Meanwood, and many of the lovely old cottages disappeared, together with the well loved Capitol cinema and ballroom. One good thing that was triggered by these events, however, was the formation of The Meanwood Village Association (M.V.A.), which you can read about on the back cover.

The photographs are a combination of those collected by the M.V.A. over the years, plus a selection of the many submitted in response to our recent appeal. Sadly, not all of them could feature in the book, but they have all been copied and will be retained in the M.V.A. archives. Many thanks to all who helped in this way.

Wherever you are in the world we hope these pictures will rekindle happy memories of Meanwood in times past.

Peter Bewell   2004

4

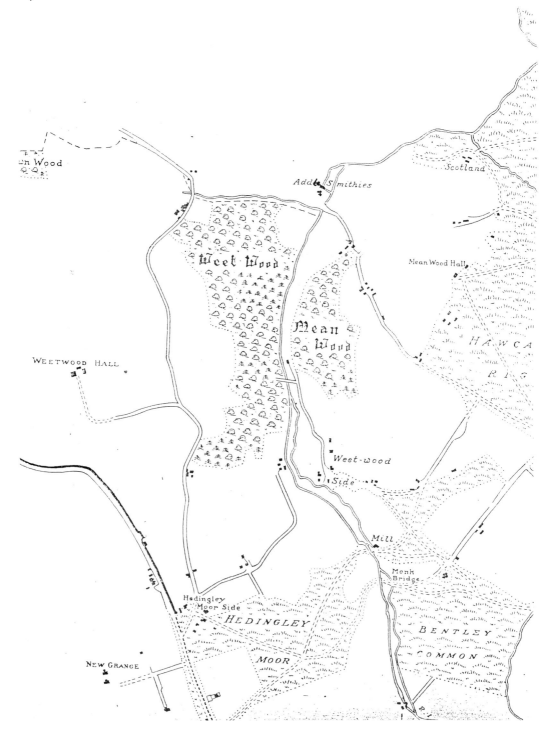

An interesting map of the area dated 1781.

A fascinating double exposure taken by himself (note the shutter release in his right hand), of the photographer Frederick Bilbrough, to whom we are indebted for a number of photographs in this book which have been printed from his old lantern slides.

Clayton's ironmongery and hardware shop which was opposite the Beckett's Arms. The lady in the doorway is Mrs. Elizabeth Clayton. In later years the shop became Crockett's Cleaners. Taken from a card posted in 1906.

Two ladies and a child in Victorian dress near Hustler's Row in 1900.

Three ladies crossing the Terminus in 1913, with the old shops in the background.

Greenwood Mount, which was built in the 1890s, showing the children in Victorian dress. The Beckett Home is seen in the background. Note the gas lamps and the unmade road.

An old sketch of "Fairfax" in Parkside Road in 1904. The artist was W. Braithwaite.

top: *The famous image of Captain Oates walking to his death in the Antarctic. Often incorrectly claimed to be a Meanwood man. He visited the area on a number of occasions, and together with his brother Bryan, inherited Meanwoodside and Ivy Cottage from his uncle Charles G.Oates.*

left: *Portrait of Captain Oates. A memorial was placed in Leeds Parish Church, and there is also a memorial tablet on the pillar at the bottom of Memorial Drive.*

below: *Memorial Inscription in Leeds Parish Church.*

*IN MEMORY OF
LAWRENCE EDWARD GRACE OATES
CAPTAIN 6th (INNISKILLING) DRAGOONS
BORN 17th MARCH 1880
WHO HAVING SERVED HIS COUNTRY WITH DISTINCTION
IN THE SOUTH AFRICAN WAR 1901-2
JOINED CAPTAIN SCOTT'S ANTARCTIC EXPEDITION 1910
REACHING THE SOUTH POLE 17th JANUARY 1912
AND ON THE RETURN JOURNEY LAT. 80°. 8′ 8″
IN THE HOPE OF SAVING THE LIVES OF HIS COMPANIONS
GAVE HIS OWN LIFE
17th MARCH 1912
THIS MONUMENT IS PLACED HERE BY FELLOW CITIZENS
AS A RECORD OF THE BRAVE ACT OF
"A VERY GALLANT GENTLEMAN"
A.D. 1913.*

A fine Victorian group, the Harburn family.
Back row; Gertrude, Robert, Agnes, Hilda.
Front row; Ellen, with Mary on her knee, Winifred, Grandma, Edith, Leonard.

Ellen and Robert Harburn in later years, with son Leonard in his First World War uniform of The South Wales Borderers.

Violet Bilbrough with Gwen in home-made push chair. 1921.
Photo; Bilbrough.

above left: *An interesting photograph, dated 1873, taken in Pietermaritzberg, South Africa. It shows W.E.Oates (back left), Francis Oates (front right), and their travelling companions, Henry Grey, T.E.Buckley and Thomas Bell, together with Francis's favourite pointer 'Rail'. Francis was determined to see the Victoria Falls, and after many problems he achieved this on the 1ˢᵗ January 1875, but sadly died of a fever 5 weeks later. 'Rail' survived, and was brought back to England where he lived another 5 years. F. and W. Oates sent 12 copies of this photograph to their brother Charles at Meanwoodside to distribute to their friends.*

above right: *Baron Moynihan of Carr Manor, K.C.M.G., C.B., D.C.L., LL.D., D.Sc., F.R.C.S. President of the Royal College of Surgeons 1926-1932.*

Taken about 1900, this scene in Highbury Lane shows the "farmyard" which later became the garage for the Warburton buses.The lady is Mrs. Warburton and the baby is Lily Warburton.
Photo; Bilbrough

A winter's morn, with the horse- drawn snowplough on Smithy Mills Lane (now the Ring Road).

Horse- drawn plough in the field in Tongue Lane which was farmed by Meanwood Park Hospital. (Now a rugby pitch). The houses in the background are Parkland Gardens.

Horse and cart on Smithy Mills Lane in almost the same spot as the snow plough.

The cottage in the woods, on the edge of the old quarry and near the Meanwood Cricket Club ground. Still very much the same today. Photo; Bilbrough.

Meanwood Hall, which was built in three phases starting in 1762, home to the Denison, Lees and Beckett families before being purchased by Leeds Corporation in 1921 to become part of the new "Meanwood Park Colony" for the mentally handicapped. Later the administration office for the Hospital Board and now up for sale.

Meanwood Towers, built in 1867, with its spectacular chimneys (which were removed in 1969). A specially built organ house housed the famous Schulze organ, which was later moved to Harrogate and then to St. Bartholomew's Church in Armley. Now converted and used as flats.

Carr Manor.
The present building was erected in 1881 on the site of a previous building known as Carr House, which had been owned and occupied by the Oates family. Purchased in 1938 by Leeds Corporation, and used as a residence for High Court Judges when sitting in Leeds.

Alder Hill off Stonegate Road was built in 1879 by Walter Rowley, a mining engineer, on land conveyed to him by his father Benjamin.
In later years converted into flats, then eventually demolished, but the Lodge and entrance gateposts are still there.

bottom: *Ivy Cottage, situated at the end of Green Road near the park, photographed in 1959. Built on part of the Mean-woodside estate which was bought by Thomas Whalley, a clothmaker, in 1696. The present house was built about 1805 by the Rinder family, and then bought by Edward Oates in 1834, eventually being inherited by Captain Oates and his brother Bryan in 1902. Occupied at one period by Alfred Elsworth, the well known Leeds artist, and later by Dr. Godfrey. Owned since 1959 by Christine and Peter Bewell.*

A view looking Westwards across Monk Bridge Road to the shop at the end of Highbury Lane.

Spring Cottage at the bottom of Monk Bridge Road. Now the Matharu general store and newsagents. For many years the well-known Gingles shop.

opposite page top: *The "Off Licence" shop halfway along Green Road. Known as Pearson's and later Pouncey's. On the left through the big wooden gates was the Hopwood poultry farm. The buildings were all demolished in the 1960s.*

opposite page bottom: *The Meanwood Post Office in 1937. It was situated at the junction of Stonegate Road and Authorpe Road, with the chemists next door. The signs indicate it also had a public telephone and a library.*

Mr. Shoesmith in the doorway of his shop in Bentley Lane.

Mr. Collin's butcher's shop in Stainbeck Avenue. Prices a bit lower than today !

McDade's "Prize Bakers" on the parade at the bottom of Stonegate Road taken at the 1953 Coronation.

Kirby's fish and chip shop in 1939, which, apart from the signs, looks very much the same as today.

The shopping parade at the bottom of Stonegate Road in 1936.
Note the big advertisement showing Albert Modley starring at the old Empire Theatre.

A charming group of children with their dolls. Violet Bilbrough is second from left.
Photo; Bilbrough

opposite page top:
An old lantern slide showing Florrie and Reg Bilbrough carrying Violet in a slung cradle.
Photo; Bilbrough.

bottom left:
Eileen Sellers (later Barratt), in her Sunday best.

bottom right:
Matt. and Fred Gildon with their toy car in the 1920s.

Children on the path into the woods near the end of Hustler's Row.

Two children seated near one of the most photographed places in Meanwood, the old bridge over Meanwood beck at the bottom of Dunny Hill. No longer there. Photo; Godfrey Bingley, 1887.

Fairfax, the old house on Parkside Road, just before the steep hill. With a datestone of 1630, one of the oldest houses in the area. In 1905 it was sold, demolished and re- erected on the same site, but at right angles to this position. The children are Rose, Reg and Johnnie Bilbrough. Photo; Bilbrough.

Parkside Road showing the 'new' Fairfax on the left and cottages on the right (long since demolished).

Parkside Road in later years, prior to refurbishment of the cottages.
Photo; Daniel.

Oddy's Fold, a row of cottages at right angles to Parkside Road. Refurbished in 2004.

A view from Parkside Road in the 1950s looking over the open fields where the Holmwood estate now stands. The farm in Church Lane can be seen in the middle distance with the Church behind, and Woodhouse Ridge in the background.
Photo; Bewell.

Another shot taken on Parkside Road with Fairfax and the cottages.

Parkside Road again, with Pauline Daniel (nee Rhodes) and John.

A building in Parkside Road with unusual windows and a nice flower garden. Photo; Daniel.

A view from the old line of the Ring Road looking over to Dunny Hill and Meanwood Grove.

The Grove on the right, with cottages in the background, one time known as Well House Inn, half-way down Dunny Hill on the sharp bends.

Another view of Well House Inn.

The 3 cottages opposite the previous photograph.

The men from the Methodist Chapel on an outing in the 1950s including Lawrence Pearson, John Barratt, Edgar Sharp, Gilbert Sellers, Leslie Rowling, Ernest Elverson, Harold Gill, Rev. Ivor Calvert, Ron Staite, W.H.Barker, Ewart Core, James Cox, Clifford Dyson, Harry Rogers, Chris Lofthouse and Geoff Barratt.

The Meanwood Snooker Club setting off on their outing outside the Beckett's Arms.

Ladies and children from the Highburys area setting off on a coach trip about 1952. Possibly organised by St. Oswald's Church.

Ladies of the British Legion on parade. Photo; Bilbrough.

An excellent photograph of the Church Sunday School Gala procession along Green Road en route to Meanwoodside. The ladies at the front are probably the Tannett-Walker sisters of Carr Manor who had church connections. Photo; Bilbrough.

A wintry scene at the weir at the bottom of the Hollies in the 1950s. Prior to the bridge being built. Photo; Bewell.

Another lovely scene from the Bilbrough collection showing the road up to the quarry and the start of the woods. Photo; Bilbrough.

The old rustic bridge at the bottom of the Hollies.

A very early picture of the 9th North West Meanwood Scout Troop with their signalling flags. The group was formed by Mr. Shoesmith before the First World War, but had to be disbanded when he and his assistant were called up for military service.

The scouts again, possibly near Ivy Cottage, where the Troop held some of their first meetings in the cellar.

Herbert Jones, affectionately known to all as "POPPA JONES". Leader of the Methodist 8th North West Leeds Scout Group from 1932 until 1966. Also Sunday School leader and tireless youth worker.

The 8th North West Leeds Scout Group and friends from the Chapel pictured at Ringways airport Manchester en route for Turnhout, in Belgium, as part of the post war scout link-ups scheme in 1949.
Back row; Marjorie Hopwood (nee Gill), Audrey Wilson, Robert Pattinson, Derek Hart, Donald Gill, Roy Berwick, Arthur Hopwood, Peter Forrestal, Barbara Gill, Betty Jones.
Front Row, Barry Kirby, Tommy Clifford, Derek Ibbetson, Mike Lalley, Peter Bewell, Colin Griffiths.
Reported to be the first time a scout group had chartered an aeroplane (an old Dakota).

The 8th North West Leeds Scout Group band setting off on their monthly parade, leading a multitude of Guides, Brownies, Scouts and Cubs around Meanwood in the late 1950s. Left to right; Colwyn Dane, Colin Naylor, Ron Jefferies, Peter Bewell, Donald Gill, Robert Pattinson, Mike Lalley, Derek Hart, Cyril Chapman, Len Lister; Brian Waterhouse and Jimmy Stringer.

Arthur Hopwood and Marjorie (nee Gill) on the steps of the Methodist Church after their wedding ceremony in 1948. The guard of honour; Left; Maurice Holl, Mike Lalley, Roy Berwick. Right; Derek Hart, Donald Gill, David Core, Peter Bewell. The little girl is Joan Elverson.

The Methodist scouts ready to set off by train to London for a sightseeing week, including watching the 1946 Victory Parade. Captured on news films sitting on the kerb opposite the Cenotaph in Whitehall.

The 8th North West Leeds Scouts in camp at Bramham Park along with the scouts from the 31st North West Leeds Group, who were based at Meanwood Park Colony. The two groups were 'twinned'.

The scout band and helpers on their Christmas carolling around Meanwood in 1950. For many years this took place in the week leading up to Christmas. Ernest Dyson, Bill Sanderson, Colin Naylor, Robert Pattinson (in Air Force uniform), Donald Gill, Barry Sanderson, Colin Griffiths, Ron Jefferies, Linda Stead and ?.

The scout band again, this time ready for inspection in the Capitol car park behind the Chapel.

The band leading the scouts, cubs, guides and brownies up the cobbled Stonegate Road.

"Meanwoodside". Erected in 1839 by Edward Oates on a site previously occupied for many years by the Whalley family. The last occupiers were Lt. Col. Edwin Kitson Clark and his wife Georgina. He died in 1942 and she in 1954 when Leeds Corporation bought the estate and, sadly, demolished the house not long afterwards.

The gardener's cottage in Meanwoodside in 1924.

Another view of "Meanwoodside" from across the beck. Although the house was demolished, the extensive grounds are now part of the very popular Meanwoodside public park.

A group at "Meanwoodside", at what appears to be a flower show. Colonel Kitson Clark is at the rear and the ladies are from the left Mrs. Wood (?), Sylvia Powys (wife of the vicar), Mrs. Kitson Clark and .....?.....

The grounds of the house were often used for community events such as church and chapel galas etc. This photograph shows a "Bonnie Babies" garden party in 1952.

Here a group of choirboys from Leeds Parish Church are assembled to sing to guests in 1926. On the left is H. Bacon Smith, the choir secretary, talking to Colonel Kitson Clark.

An interior shot of the house. What a shame it was demolished !

A postcard from 1911 showing the view from Woodhouse Ridge looking down on Boothroyd's Mill and dam. The Yorkshire Switchgear was later built on this site.

centre: *Another postcard, this time looking at the Ridge from the slopes of Sugarwell Hill, on what is now the Urban Farm. The neatly laid out Ridge footpaths can clearly be seen, together with the allotment plots. Houses in Woodhouse and a Church (possibly Wrangthorn) can be seen in the background. Date of photograph unknown, but one of the newly built "White Houses" can be seen on the extreme right.*

Woodhouse Ridge, Leeds.

The third postcard shows the scene along one of the top footpaths with the bandstand, a popular venue for Sunday and holiday concerts. Date unknown, but no 1920s " White Houses" can be seen.

A delightful scene of the crowds around the bandstand. Sugarwell Hill is on the opposite side of the valley with the extensive rhubarb fields. On the right is the destructor chimney (waste incineration plant).

An old print showing the Boothroyd dam and mill. Later the site of Bullus's Dyeworks and the Yorkshire Switchgear.

Looking down on Bullus's Dyeworks, with Meanwood Road and some new 'White Houses' in the background.

Woodland Dyeworks and adjacent cottages at the bottom of the Ridge, with the nursery gardens in the foreground.

The infants class at Green Road School seated at their wooden desks in 1932.

Children celebrating Empire Day in 1931 in the playground at Green Road School.

Children of 1889 outside Green Road School.

A large group of children in the field behind the school about 1912. The Beckett Home can be seen in the background.

Children of Standard 3 outside Green Road School in 1921.

Reading time for the children in the area beneath the belltower.

A photograph taken in Green Road outside the school. The building on the left was part of the Meanwoodside estate and is now the Parks Department store. On the right, a lady can be seen leaving the little shop and cottages. This spot is now the entrance to the school upper play-ground which was built on the former tennis courts.

Hollin Lane Farm, on the site of the Whalley Tannery. It was there in the middle of the 17th century, and was probably the oldest tannery in Meanwood. This part was converted to a dwelling house in the late 1970s.

The Infants class at Bentley Lane School about 1932. The children include Donald Clifford, Keith Collins, Audrey Horsefield, Frances Parsons, Margaret Barnes, Betty Gardener and Pauline Phipps. Note the desks, dolls house, dolls bed, and the little dolls in the children's hands.

A boys class outside Bentley Lane School about 1931. Back row; John Vollans, Harry Proctor, ...Buckley, ...Clarkson (?) Jack Berry, Henry Websdale, Willie Drake, Sidney Holstead, Gordon Rounhill, ... Levett.

Middle row; ...Lane (?), Vincent Combes, Desmond Bullock, Douglas Wright, Bernard Poyser, ...Newton, Tommy Hoare, ..?.., Colin Brindley, ...Rothwell.

above:
The original Methodist Chapel built in 1811 at the bottom of Church Lane. After the present chapel was built in 1881 this building became the Meanwood Laundry, later Pick's Builders Merchants, then Acorn Glass and now awaiting redevelopment as dwellings.
Photo; Bewell.

The 1811 datestone over the entrance to the Laundry taken in the 1950s.
Photo; Bewell.

The wedding of Enid Hepworth and David Bishop in the 1960s in the present Meanwood Chapel. Since then the organ console, choir stalls and pulpit have been moved to new positions.
Photo; Bewell.

MEANWOOD METHODIST CHURCH, LEEDS.

Opening and Dedication of the Organ

SATURDAY, 19th DECEMBER, 1953

The programme for the dedication of the new organ in 1953.

The ladies of the Chapel choir on an outing in 1916. The young lady in the centre is Edna Turner (later Sellers).

below: Chapel Sunday School anniversary concert about 1912.

A group of people from the chapel on holiday in Whitby in 1948.
One of the many holidays organised by 'Poppa' Jones at Christian Endeavour Holiday Homes.

Another of 'Poppa' Jones' holidays, this time at Troon in Scotland in the 1950s.

The Methodist youth club on a hike in the 1950s. There was an organised hike every Bank Holiday Monday for many years.
Photo; Bewell.

The Chapel square dance team organised by Harold Gill (centre back).

The Rev. Stanley Rose, the Meanwood Methodist Minister in the 1960s.
He later became the Chairman of the Leeds District.
Photo; Bewell.

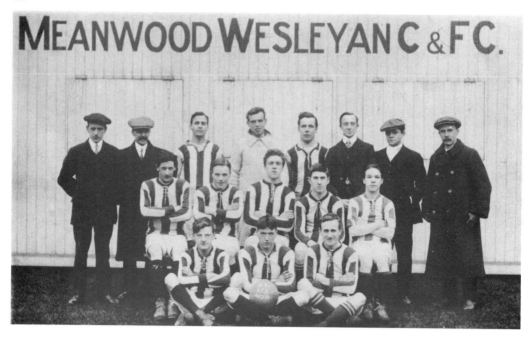

Meanwood Wesleyan football team of 1912/13.
Back; Alvra Hopwood, Herbert Hindes, Herbert Mercer, William Hopwood, C.Ibbetson,
H.Spencer, A..Bowman, Chris Lofthouse.
Centre; F.Wright, E.Runton, E.Binns, A.Ellis, C.Roberts.
Front; G.Simpson, S.Costello, Sam Hopwood.

The Chapel football team in the 1920s with their supporters.

The Chapel football team in the 1950s.
Back; ..?........., .?. Fletcher, Roger Hall, ...?......, Brian Walker, ...?......,
Front; Peter Bewell, Ken Brown, Warren Scholey, Syd Collier, Barry Walker.

The arch rivals in the Leeds Allied Churches League! Meanwood Trinity.
Back; Mel Downham, Elwyn Owen, Alan Cordingley, Pete Allison.
Front; Andy Mitchell, Fred James, Laurie Crampton, Bill Peters, Billy Hill, Mick Dagley, Jack
Desadeler.

A view of the Parish Church taken from what is now Church Avenue.

The Church, viewed from Green Road, looking up Memorial Drive. A line of trees was planted on either side of the Drive (some can be seen on the left) after the First World War, in memory of servicemen who lost their lives. The war memorial can be seen on the front left. The tablet to Captain Oates is on the right hand pillar. Although the Drive was built over with sheltered housing and flats in the late 1970s, it still retains the name Memorial Drive and some of the trees have survived.

An interior view of the Church.

The scene at the Lych Gate in 1946 or 1947 showing the choirboys with the organist and choirmaster Mr. Parker.

Church Wardens, Jim Spencer and Arthur Thackray.

The Vicars of Meanwood;
Above; Rev. George Urquhart 1849-50, Rev. David Mappleton 1851-1883, Rev. H. Annesley Powys 1883-1917.
Below; Rev. R.B. McKee 1918-1933, Rev. R.C. Shuttleworth 1933- 1944, Rev.J.M. Borrow 1944-55.

opposite page top: *Dignitaries at the laying of the Parochial Hall foundation stone on the 25th May 1935. Lord Moynihan, The Bishop of Knaresborough The Rt. Rev. Paul Fulgrave Delacour De Labilliere, the Chaplain, The Rev. J. Philips, Lady Moynihan, Canon S.H.Harris and the Rev. R.B. McKee.*

bottom left: *Rev. S. Brown, Vicar 1955-64.*

centre and bottom right: *Dignitaries at the opening of the Parochial Hall on the 28th September 1935. The lady who performed the opening ceremony was Lady Nussey.*

Welcome home party for ex-servicemen in the Parochial Hall in May 1947.

Mrs. Shuttleworth, the wife of the Vicar, in the Parochial Hall with a group of ladies making items for the Red Cross in 1940.

A crowded Hall at the Centenary celebrations in 1949.

The ceremony at the opening of the new path.

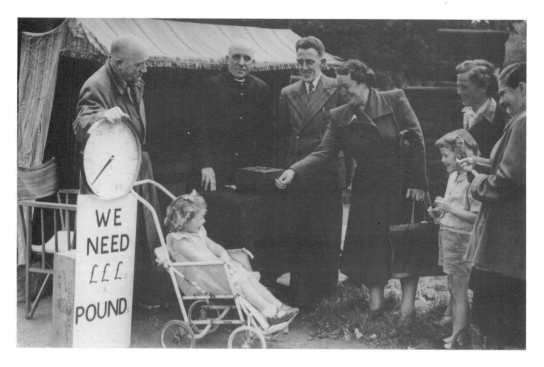

Gift day in 1954 with the Rev. John Borrow and church wardens Norman Grose and Arthur Thackray.

A group taken in the Bowoods. The lady in the centre with the baby, together with the girl in front, had been evacuated to Meanwood from London to escape the doodlebug attacks towards the end of the Second World War. Dorothy Thackray (later Fenton) is on the right.

Dorothy Thackray again, this time all dressed up as a bridesmaid at the wedding of Frank and Mattie Rhodes on the 1st of August 1928.

A wedding group outside the Parochial Hall in 1937 (?) The happy couple were Jack Fozzard and Freda Dagless. Her father, the man in the dark suit, was Mr. Dagless a Meanwood farmer.

The Rev.R.C. Shuttleworth talking to a group of gentlemen on the memorial seat.

Dennis Rudland appearing as the dame in the pantomime Aladdin in the Parochial Hall about 1948.

The old Meanwood Vicarage, demolished about 1964 to make way for the new one.

The Bay Horse on Parkside Road. The pub is still there, but the three cottages on the left have been demolished.
Photo; Daniel.

Henry Wiggins with his cows at the back of the Bay Horse before it was extended.

William Wiggins, the grandson of Henry, on the doorstep of his house, which had a dairy beneath in what is now part of the Bay Horse car park.

The original Beckett's Arms at the terminus.

A very mixed group outside the Myrtle on Parkside Road.

A Warburton bus, which ran a service between Leeds and Harrogate in 1921. Albert Warburton garaged his vehicles in Highbury Lane and the drivers and conductors had to service their own buses. The licence cost two shillings and sixpence!
Photo; Bilbrough.

A 1908 shot of a tram, with an open front and back on the top deck, standing at the terminus outside the Beckett's Arms, whilst the overhead trolley was changed round.

A No. 8 tram in 1949, which ran between Meanwood and Elland Road.

A 45 single decker bus on the Meanwood to Wortley Route. The Capitol Cinema is in the background with an advertisement for "Ramsbottom Rides Again", starring Arthur Askey.

A 1950 shot of a double decker bus at the stop outside Bateson's Tannery in Green Road.

Six men of the National Fire Service, ("N.F.S.") on parade in the Capitol car park in 1941. Their base was the Snow White Laundry in Authorpe Road. Their equipment seemed to consist of one car with some ladders, a towed pump and a bike!

The Meanwood Air Raid Wardens 1939/45.

Sydney Noel "Bob" Ellison outside 56, Greenwood Mount, dressed in his air raid warden's uniform. He was the electrician and projectionist at the Capitol Cinema and Ballroom for many years.

The Capitol Picture House (opened in 1922) in Green Road and the parade of shops. The entrance to the Ballroom was next to the far shop. The corner of the chapel garden wall can be seen on the left, together with a number of interesting old cars on the forecourt. The buildings were demolished in 1980 to be replaced by a supermarket, shops and bank.

Stonegate Road with its cobbles and old cars in 1950. Dagless's farm is the white building in the centre.

Looking across the terminus. The Chapel entrance on the left, Bateson's Tannery in the background and, behind the trees on the right was the Geisha Tea Gardens. The tram lines show that the trams originally went up Stonegate Road a little way. The gentlemen standing in the road certainly wouldn't be able to do that today!
Photo; Bilbrough.

Kent House, at the junction of Stainbeck Avenue and Stonegate Road. It was where the steps up to the shopping area now stand.

REVOLUTION WELL, MEANWOOD. 229.

Bog in the adjoining field drained.
Spring opened and conducted hither.
For the benefit of the passenger and the neighbouring house,
November 5th, 1788.

The 100th Anniversary from the landing of King William,
In memory of which happy era this is. by Joseph Oates,
inscribed the " Revolution Well."

Revolution Well in Stonegate Road. It is still there at the bottom of Parkland Crescent.

King Alfred's Castle on the hill between Stonegate Road and Tongue Lane. Taken in 1930.

An old shot of the Seven Arches with people walking across the top.

Another shot of the arches, this time with Pauline Daniel and Susan walking across, 1958. Later, railings were erected to stop people doing this. Although not on film, it was a schoolboy 'dare' to ride ones bike across!
Photo; Daniel.

Two gentlemen taking it easy at King Alfred's Castle. The folly was finally demolished in 1946, having become unsafe following the ravages of time.

Scotland Mill cottages, which were on the route to the Seven Arches, just to the north of the Ring Road. Now demolished.

Another view of Scotland Mill cottages.

Myrtle Square cottages. Photo; Daniel.

Myrtle Square again. Photo; Daniel.

This time the Myrtle Tavern can be seen on the right. The field in the foreground is now part of the Holmwood estate. Photo; Daniel.

A 1922 photograph of the Meanwood estate, said to be built as 'homes for heroes' from the war. They were known as the 'White Houses', and were demolished about 1988-90 to make way for a new estate. Woodhouse cricket field can be seen in the foreground, with the 'pavilion' near the bottom.

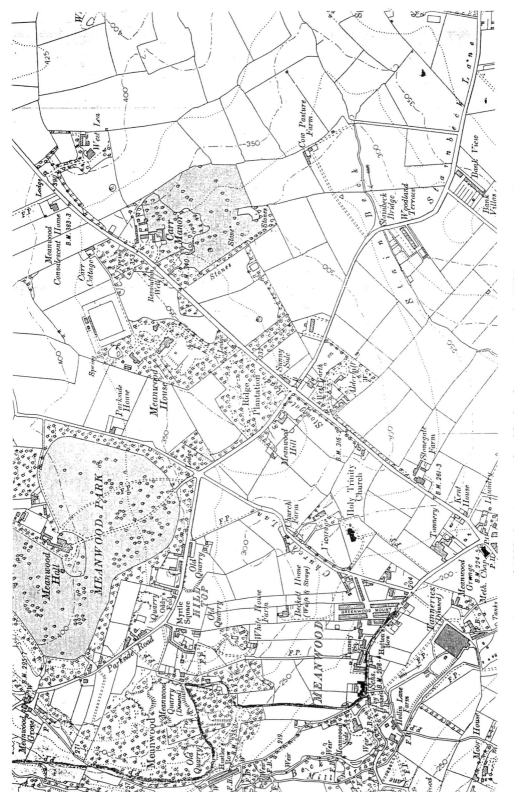

A map of 1909 showing considerable development since the 1781 map on page 4.

An excited group of children, from the Bentley's and Monkbridge's, preparing the bonfire in 1936. They included Tommy and Mary Clifford, Joyce Prill, Joyce Spencer, June Sunley, Raymond Risingham, Maurice Dales, Howard Thorpe, Rene Prill, Kenneth Riley, Keith Collins, Bobby Danby, Eric Clifford, Gladys Staveley.

This Yorkshire Post photograph was captioned, "The girl on the log is no chump". In fact it was Tommy Clifford! Other children included Eric Clifford, Maurice Dales, Bobby Danby, ..?.. Copson, and Kenneth Riley who was killed in the war.

A rather stern looking group of workers, probably at one of the tanneries.

Seven lady workers, with the proprietor (believed to be Mr. R.J. Fardell), outside the small pre-1914 laundry in Brookfield Road. The building was much later used as a joiners shop and it is still there.

Two gentlemen having a breather and a pipe during haymaking.

A busy working group in the hayfield.

Workers David Fielding (front) and Mick Hilton in the tannery. A rather smelly and messy job. Depending on the wind direction, the smell from the tannery would often permeate the whole area. Although commonly known as The Tannery, no tanning has taken place there since 1904. After that date it was fellmongering, which is concerned with the removal and washing of the wool.

Another worker sorting the wool. A newspaper article said that the cricket pitch at Highbury Works (which is still in use) was built on Australian soil, because the cleanings from the sheepskins, which were imported from Australia, were used as filling when the pitch was created.

Workers outside the tannery. Obviously a major employer in days past. Work finally finished in the 1990s, and all the stone buildings were converted into dwellings.

94

A happy group at the Methodist Sunday School Carnival in Meanwoodside June 18th 1949. From the left; Anne Ludbrook, Margaret Lumley, Kathleen Page, Linda Stead (the Queen), Billy Simpson, Jean Marsden, Dianne Fowlis, Diana Stead.

The procession, en route to Crabtree's sports ground, in 1962, with some grand old cars. They are passing the bottom of Church Avenue, and Bateson's Tannery can be seen in the background.

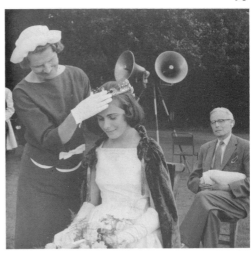

The 1961 Queen, Patricia Shilleto, being crowned by Mrs. Olver. Dr. R.H.Olver is seated on the right.

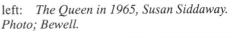

left: *The Queen in 1965, Susan Siddaway. Photo; Bewell.*

In 1950 Sylvia Thackray was Queen, and is seen here making her speech at Meanwoodside.

Timothy Holland, a happy cub, who had won first prize in the children's cake baking competition. At the microphone is Joe Mayne the Sunday School Superintendent.

96

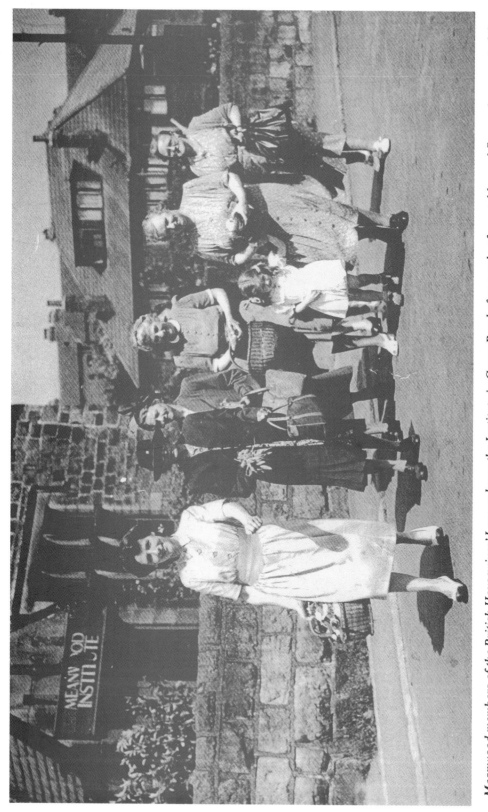

Meanwood members of the British Housewives' League leave the Institute in Green Road after a sale of vegetables and flowers in support of the campaign for cheaper produce, about 1950. The lady on the left is Mrs. Sledge (nee Holliday). The little girl who is her daughter, is holding grandma's hand.

A lovely old photograph showing the cottages adjoining the Institute in Green Road with their well- stocked gardens. Note the old Co-op and Tannery Square, together with the old lady extreme left. The cottages were demolished to make way for Sunset Road.

A wedding group outside the Institute in Green Road. The groom was Edward Hill. Note the sign in the window for 'The Meanwood Adult School'.

An intriguing 1914 picture of a wedding group, which appears to be taken in a quarry. The happy couple were Rose Bilbrough and Arthur Major. Weeks later, Arthur was killed on active service in France. Photo; Bilbrough.

A large group outside the Institute. Obviously some sort of celebration, as the lady in the centre is holding a cake. Photo; Bilbrough.

Meanwood Church of England School in Green Road, which was built in 1840. Note there is no upstairs classroom on the left. This was added in 1912. Obviously taken before the houses opposite were built in the late 1920s.

Daisy Bank, the large house at the bottom of Church Lane, just before demolition. Green Close was then built on the site about 1960.
Photo; Bewell.

Hollin House, which technically is in Headingley, being just over the beck, was opposite Meanwoodside. It was owned by the Oates family for many years and considered to be part of the Meanwood scene. Taken about 1900. The gentleman in the top hat, with his wife and dog, was probably the owner or tenant. The group on the right with the lawnmower was Mr. Hudson, the gardener, with his family. The ladies in the doorway were, apparently, the servants.

Highbury Works Cricket Club, originally formed by the tannery and still going strong. Their team of the late 1940s, seen here, included Jim Moulton, Freddie Beck, Tug Wilson, and Ken Burnett (Captain).

An old gentleman standing near the far end of Hustler's Row on the path into the woods.

Oates Cottages in 1917. Later demolished. The site is now occupied by the children's playground near the entrance to Meanwoodside.

103

Hustler's Row, with smoking coal fires and well cultivated gardens. Still there, being a much sought after location in the woods.

*above: Bateson's
Tannery in Green
Road in the 1950s.
Today the site of the
Netto supermarket
and shops.
Photo; Bewell.*

*The old cottages in
Providence Square
near Church Lane,
prior to demolition in
the 1960s.
Photo; Bewell.*

Bywater Buildings facing the entrance to the park off Green Road. They survived the demolition blitz. Photo; Daniel.

Brick Row at the bottom of Church Lane, built in 1847 by James Martin the Meanwood papermaker, as an investment for his three daughters. Now the site of flats known as Church Lane Mews. Very unusual, being built in brick, in an otherwise all stone village. Note the 'coal holes' in the boundary wall. Photo; Bewell.

The Beckett Home at the top of Greenwood Mount, which was built in 1886 to house 28 girls classed as 'waifs and strays'. One of the main benefactors was Miss Mary Beckett of Somerby Park, Gainsborough. Converted to a nursery for 30 babies in 1935 under the control of the Church of England Children's Society. In 1950 Leeds Corporation took it over, then sold it for conversion into private flats in the 1960s.

Staff and children from the nursery.

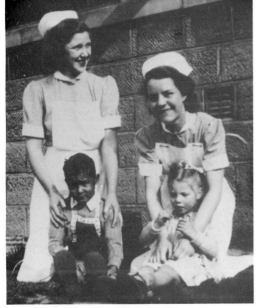

above: A seated lady who worked at the Home.

top left: Three happy kiddies from the nursery.

Two of the nurses with their charges.

More children outside the nursery.

Potternewton Lane in 1933. The trees on the skyline were known as the 'Seven Sisters'. They disappeared when the Beck Hill housing estate was built. The hillside was widely cultivated as allotments.

A winter's day in Meanwood with the Tannery and dam in the foreground. Probably in the 1960s.

A procession winding its way up the original Church Lane.

The Yorkshire Penny Bank when it was at 575 Meanwood Road. Note the shiny little savings boxes in the window. Later used as a doctor's surgery, a medical deputising service and then business premises.

Cottages 35-41 off the steep part of Church Lane.

Nos 31 and 33 Church Lane, just below the previous photograph. 31 was the home of Marjorie and Arthur Hopwood. Demolished about 1964.

An interior view of the Yorkshire Switchgear and Engineering Co. in Meanwood Road in the 1940s. A major employer in the area. The factory was demolished to make way for more housing in the 1990s.

A 1906 photograph of Meanwood Road with the tram lines and cobbles.

A family outside Oakfield Cottage. The house had to be demolished to make way for the new Grove Lane. The family were rehoused in the new house seen on the right of the picture below.

Grove Lane under construction.

Procession of ex-servicemen crossing the terminus. The gentleman in the front centre is Mr. Shoesmith. Probably on Remembrance Sunday in the 1920s.

Lads of the 31st Leeds Company of the Boys' Brigade pictured in the Church grounds, with the Church Avenue houses in the background. Dennis Rudiand is the lad behind the drum and on his right is the captain Keith Lister.

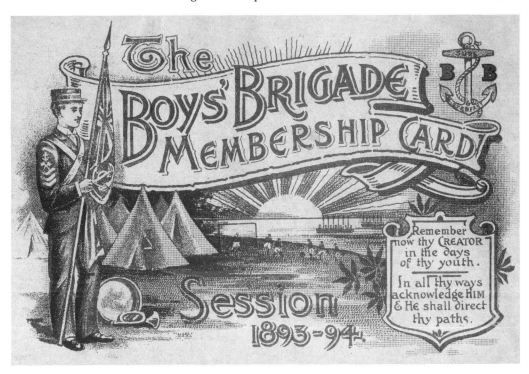

Roland Worth's Boys' Brigade Membership card for 1893-94. He was a sergeant in squad no. 3 of the 2nd Leeds Company which was formed on the 21st October 1892 at Meanwood Wesleyan Chapel. Sadly, Roland was killed in the First World War.

Brownies and Guides from the Methodist Chapel in the late 1940s. Including Kathleen Best, Linda Stead, Eileen Sellers, Margaret Mabb, Pauline Rhodes, Hilda Sharp, June Raistrick, Margaret Dyson, Margaret Naylor, Diana Stead, Shirley Ingle, Mary Bell, Hazel Hill, Valerie Stead and Christine Bentley.

The 1ˢᵗ Meanwood Guide Company (from the Church) passing the saluting base in Roundhay Park Arena, in June 1943.

Construction of an air raid shelter at the destructor site in Meanwood Road, November 14th 1938.

The destructor chimney and matching poplar trees in the 1950s. Rhubarb fields in the background and the housing on the top of Sugarwell Hill. Photo; Bewell.

A rather hazy photograph, but a very interesting one. It shows the Hindenberg airship passing over Stainbeck Road in 1936. Photo; Hill.

The "Meanwood" public house at the junction of Meanwood Road and Grove Lane. Demolished in 2000 and replaced by flats.

Violet Bilbrough on her scooter behind her house, 26 Greenwood Mount, in 1918. The row of houses behind was Green Row. Photo; Bilbrough.

Two of the Bilbrough children behind Greenwood Mount. The old chapel is in the background. Photo; Bilbrough.

A charming shot of Althea M. White on her first day at Bentley Lane School in 1956.

122

An aerial photograph of the Meanwood Park Hospital site. Meanwood Towers and the Parklands can be discerned in the top left, and on the top right you can see the Parksides, whilst the Bay Horse and Oddy's Fold can just be seen on the right.

Another aerial shot, this time showing the Church in centre left, the farm in Church Lane later to become the Holmwood estate. In the far distance the fields are where the Moortown estate was built. Probably taken in the 1930s.

Demolition of Dr. Lister's House and surgery in Meanwood Road in the 1950s or 60s. Near the present Lloyds Pharmacy. Photo; Bewell.

The final days of the cottages in Hutton's Row off Green Road (behind Greenwood Mount). Another victim of the demolition craze of the 1960s. Photo; Bewell.